Original title:
A Taste of Island Life

Copyright © 2025 Creative Arts Management OÜ
All rights reserved.

Author: Vivian Laurent
ISBN HARDBACK: 978-1-80581-643-0
ISBN PAPERBACK: 978-1-80581-170-1
ISBN EBOOK: 978-1-80581-643-0

Reflections in a Hammock

Swinging lazily, my drink in hand,
The world drifts by, oh so unplanned.
A snack in my lap, it slips and slides,
Cats steal my chips, oh what a ride!

Birds sing a tune, I hum along,
With waves like a choir, singing my song.
The breeze gives my belly a playful poke,
As laughter ensues, a hammock's no joke!

Sunrise Over the Mangroves

The sun pops up like a jolly old friend,
Wakes the sleeping crabs, it's a race to the end.
I spill my coffee, it splashes quite wide,
While a parrot chuckles, perched with pride.

The early joggers, in their mismatched gear,
Dodge puddles and flip-flops, it's a comedic sphere.
The mangroves sway, in gossip they share,
While I trip on my shoelace, flailing in air!

Colorful Markets and Local Lores

In the market square, there's a lovely bazaar,
Colorful spices peeking from each jar.
I bartered a coconut, two dollars or so,
The seller just winked, 'You're too slow, too slow!'

Local legends spill like the fruits on display,
About mermaids or pirates who danced by the bay.
I listen and giggle, with eyes wide and bright,
As folks sell me tales, like they'd sell me a kite!

Coastal Dreams of a Salted Past

Sandy toes and giggles, memories grow,
With each playful wave, secrets to show.
I chased a seagull, thought it was my mate,
But it snagged my sandwich, oh how it ate!

We built up a castle, yet it crumbled down,
A tide came in, what a mischievous clown!
With salty air kisses and sun-soaked cheer,
The coastal tales whispered, draw us all near.

Seagrape Dreams Under the Open Sky

In hammocks hung, we sway and swing,
The seagrapes laugh, oh what joy they bring.
A crab in shades, with swagger, slides,
Claiming the beach, where secret fun resides.

With salty curls, we shuffle our feet,
Chasing flip-flops down the sandy street.
A gull steals fries with expert flair,
While we just giggle, without a care.

Horizons Painted with Tropical Hues

The sunset spills like a melting crayon,
As we argue if it's orange or a mauve dawn.
In coconut hats, we strut around,
Pretending we're kings, with laughter abound.

A parrot squawks the latest jokes,
While we munch on fish and dance like folks.
Waves crash, and so does our mood,
As we trip on seaweed, that slippery food.

Cascades of Culture in Coastal Breath

Island tunes play as the conch-shell blows,
While tourists try hula, but trip on their toes.
A festival feast, with conch fritters galore,
As we dance like dolphins on the sandy shore.

Cowrie shells clink, in rhythm they rhyme,
We worry 'bout sunburn, but are lost in time.
With every sip of rum, our worries fade,
As the locals tease the uncoordinated parade.

Laughter Echoes in Island Breezes

Tiki torches flicker, casting silly shadows,
As we swap stories like excited sparrows.
A lizard dashes, stealing the show,
As we all laugh at its ungraceful flow.

The dog runs by, with a coconut prize,
And we cheer it on with wide-open eyes.
Under the stars, with bright island cheer,
Life feels like a carnival, oh so dear.

Serene Shores of Seaglass Serenity

On beaches where the seaglass shines,
I trip over a crab that whines.
The sun's a clown, so bright and bold,
While flip-flops fly, their stories told.

A hammock swings, but waits in vain,
My coconut drink spills like a rain.
With laughter loud, the folks nearby,
Try surfing on the seagull's cry.

Coconut Breeze and Coral Skies

A coconut falls, it's hard as stone,
I try to catch it, can't quite own.
Tropical birds squawk like a band,
While I just sit here, drink in hand.

With coral skies, the day's a tease,
The fishes laugh under the breeze.
They say, 'Silly human, take a dive!'
I splash about—oh, how I thrive!

Sunset Serenade on Sandy Shores

Sunset drips like melted gold,
As I try to dance, feeling bold.
The crabs join in with sideways moves,
While beach balls fly and laughter grooves.

With every wave, a giggle spills,
The sand gets stuck—I've lost my thrills.
The ocean sings a silly tune,
While I just hope to dodge that moon!

Island Secrets in the Twilight Glow

In twilight glow, the secrets stay,
As I trip on shells in a goofy sway.
The palms are swaying, trying to dance,
While I wave back—not a second chance.

The stars peep out, all grins and winks,
As I pour lemonade in the sink.
The fish tease me, 'Come take a swim!'
I'll stick to snacks, on that I'm grim!

Before the Storm: Island Reflections

The coconut fell, oh what a sight,
It rolled away, gave quite a fright.
The crabs dart by, in sync they scurry,
While seagulls laugh, they always hurry.

Morning's sun paints the sand so bright,
While fishermen wrestle, what a fight!
The boats all bob, they dance and sway,
And sharks might giggle, 'Not today!'

Tides of Time: An Island Reverie

The tide rolls in, bringing flip-flops,
A fashion choice that never stops.
Sandy dogs chase waves with glee,
Splashing around, so wild and free.

Palm trees sway, a show on repeat,
While locals dance to a rhythm, quite neat.
A parrot squawks, a cheeky sound,
Who knew fun could be so profound?

Samba of the Shoreline: A Dance of Waves

The waves hit hard, like an ocean's kiss,
Beach balls fly, not a moment to miss.
Tanning oils, they glisten and glow,
While surfers catch rides, putting on a show.

Sunset brings laughter, so bright and bold,
With fishy tales of adventures retold.
The nighttime comes with stars that twinkle,
And crickets chirp with a rhythmic crinkle.

Shells and Shadows of Forgotten Times

Shells scattered wide, a treasure trove,
Of stories whispered, where secrets rove.
Footprints lead to a party scene,
Where beach balls bounce like a jellybean.

Old shipwrecks tell of times so grand,
Yet here we are with a cold drink in hand.
As shadows stretch under the moon's glow,
We dance with laughter, putting on a show.

Melodies of the Mariner's Heart

A sailor sings off-key,
With seagulls in the fray.
His boat a floating pub,
Where fish join in the play.

The waves dance like they're drunk,
Each splash a hearty cheer.
Crabs tap-dance in the sand,
While sharks just grin from ear.

A coconut's a bard,
That tells tales of the sea.
But every time it speaks,
It sounds like garbled tea.

With laughter on the breeze,
And sunburns in the mix,
These tales of joy and jest,
Are sailor's silly tricks.

Driftwood Dreams and Ocean Tides

Driftwood sits up proud,
A throne for crabs and snails.
Each wave whispers secrets,
While seaweed tells its tales.

The tides come and they go,
Like friends at a wild party.
Starfish wear silly hats,
While clams play cards all hearty.

Seashells sing out loud,
Like sirens on a spree.
But one got lost in gossip,
And now can't find the sea.

Together they unite,
In this sandy parade.
With laughter swirling 'round,
Life's a wacky charade.

Tidepools of Reflection and Reverie

In tidepools, life's a show,
Where shrimp do funny prance.
And anemones wave hands,
Like they're in a dance.

Small fish gossip away,
About the crabs next door.
While sea stars eat some chips,
Just looking to explore.

A tiny octopus,
Wears a hat that's too big.
It slips into the tide,
And throws a little jig.

Amidst the bubbling joy,
Where sea glass cuts the light,
These pools of dreams delight,
With laughter day and night.

Crickets Sing as the Sun Sets

As the sun dips low,
The crickets start their jam.
With frogs in concert too,
A quirky little slam.

Their chorus fills the night,
With tunes so out of tune.
The fish roll their fishy eyes,
While dolphins dance in swoon.

The stars above all giggle,
As they twinkle with delight.
This symphony of nonsense,
Makes even owls take flight.

With laughter 'neath the moon,
And shadows being silly,
Nature holds a comedy,
That tickles every silly.

Exotic Fruits and Floating Wishes

In the market, mangoes wink,
Papayas giggle, what do you think?
Coconuts rolling, having a race,
Bananas in hammocks, taking a rest.

Pineapple hats on silly heads,
Limes that dance on gingerbread.
Strawberries whisper, 'Life is sweet!'
Watermelons chasing, quick on their feet.

Guava twirled in a fruity dance,
Fruit flies chuckle, seizing the chance.
Kiwi in shades, looking so cool,
While coconut crabs play it like a jewel.

Juggling the flavors, a fruity spree,
Tasting the laughter, so carefree.
Floating wishes on waves of delight,
Enjoying the antics under the light.

Dances Under the Tropical Moon

Beneath the moon, crabs take a chance,
Holding their pincers, ready to dance.
Turtles are twirling, a slow, silly groove,
While feisty iguanas join in the move.

Frogs on a lily pad sing out of tune,
Bouncing together, a wild afternoon.
An octopus joins, waving eight arms,
While dolphins dive down, oh, what charms!

Palm trees sway with arms wide and free,
Throwing shade on a dance party spree.
A parrot squawks, "Let's have some fun!"
While the island laughs, till the night is done.

By morning, they'll rest, all tuckered out,
With dreams full of giggles, no room for doubt.
The tropical moon has brought them such joy,
Dancing creatures, every girl, and boy.

Rustling Leaves and Ocean Echoes

The leaves are gossiping, sharing the news,
About the sea turtles in their new shoes.
A breeze whispers secrets, giggles in the air,
While the ocean echoes, "Who's got a dare?"

Nuts rolling downhill, playing tag with the tide,
Squirrels are laughing, trying to hide.
Clams holding court at a long sandy table,
Shells like hats, feeling quite stable.

Waves tickle toes, daring them to play,
Seagulls are squawking, "Hey! Who's got hay?"
Seashells gossip, spiral tales of the day,
Every rustle and splash, a grand cabaret.

Breezes turn whispers into sandy flights,
Filling the island with giggly delights.
Amidst these sounds, a laughter parade,
Rustling leaves with ocean's serenade.

The Heartbeat of the Island

In the island's heart, a rhythm's alive,
With roosters crowing, they take a dive.
Chickens in bow ties strut through the yard,
While lizards are racing with smiles from the start.

The fish swim by with fins that shine,
While sunbathers giggle, sipping divine.
The wind tells jokes, rustling the trees,
While coconuts pondering, "What's with the breeze?"

Crabs tap dance on rocks with flair,
Sea stars clapping, filled with good air.
The island beats on, a funny old tune,
Under the gaze of a bright, chubby moon.

Such is the life where giggles abound,
With whispers and waves, joyous sounds surround.
In the island's heartbeat, all's bright and wild,
Where laughter grows, forever beguiled.

Tents and Tales Under Starry Nights

Beneath a sky with twinkling lights,
We pitched our tents, like clumsy sights.
A raccoon danced, thinking it was slick,
While we all laughed, and found it quick.

S'mores gone rogue, with chocolate spills,
Our laughter echoed, through the hills.
The fire crackled, with stories spun,
We looked for ghosts, which turned to fun.

The night grew old, but jokes reigned bright,
We drew on tales, staying up all night.
The stars above were twinkling bold,
With every tale, new laughter unfolded.

The morning sun brought sleepy eyes,
We stumbled out to bright blue skies.
With sandy toes and giddy grins,
Awakening to joy, the real win begins.

Captured Moments in a Coastal Canvas

A canvas broad, with splashes bright,
We painted joys, with pure delight.
Seagulls squawked, stealing our fries,
While painters laughed at their surprise.

With brushes brisk, we colored the sea,
A dolphin leapt, as if to agree.
But ocean waves, oh they conspired,
To wash away what we admired.

We snapped our photos, silly poses,
With crab in hand, we struck a rose.
The backdrop changed to playtime fun,
As tides chased down our laughter's run.

Later we feasted on fishy fare,
With salty jokes that filled the air.
In every snapshot, joy got ensnared,
As memories shimmered, laughter shared.

Serendipitous Swells of Comfort

On surfboards high, we lost our grip,
The waves became a wild trip.
Riding swells with splashes loud,
Like cartoon fish, we flipped and bowled.

The lifeguard laughed, he raised his brow,
As I tumbled in, oh, take a bow!
The waters' laughter pulled me in,
To join the dance, a splashy win.

With coconut drinks, we chilled with glee,
Swimsuits mismatched, a sight to see.
The sun would slide, like buttercream,
Our day of waves, a waking dream.

As twilight fell, we built a fire,
With tales of waves and buoyant desire.
Our hearts were full, with silly smiles,
Content together, a few more miles.

Marinated by the Caribbean Sun

The sun beat down, a golden crown,
We sizzled bright, no need to frown.
With sunscreen slathered, like icing sweet,
We laughed as crabs scuttled on their feet.

Mango shakes in hand, we dared to sip,
And danced like fools, let happiness flip.
The reggae tunes swayed hips and feet,
As laughter rolled like waves, so neat.

A pineapple hat, oh what a sight,
We wore it proud with all our might.
The conch shells blew, with noises strange,
In a world where normal felt quite deranged.

As sunsets glowed, the colors were wild,
We wiggled and giggled, like a child.
With laughter strong and hearts so light,
We embraced the night, till morning light.

Dancing with the Tides of Time

The waves rolled in with laughs so bright,
As seagulls danced in silly flight.
Old men in boats cast lines so long,
They tangled up with a fishy song.

Flip-flops flopped on sandy shores,
While kids built castles, ignored chores.
The sun set low, the skies ablaze,
As beach balls flew in chaotic ways.

Crabs did the cha-cha on the sand,
With every wave, they took a stand.
A picnic basket spilled its treats,
Fruit salad with some sandy feats.

So raise a glass to days so bright,
Where time just dances, oh what a sight!
We'll laugh and cheer, forget the clock,
In this silly world, let's just unlock.

Essence of Mangoes and Memories

A mango tree wears its golden crown,
While kids below they twist and frown.
Juice drips down like summer rain,
And sticky hands are part of the game.

We chase the fruit that rolls away,
The neighbors share and laugh and play.
A dog steals one, the chase is on,
We giggle loud 'til the day is gone.

In the shade, we trade our tales,
Of pirate ships and treasure sails.
The laughter bubbles, stories soar,
Sweet mangoes eaten, always more!

So let's throw a party, mango delight,
With ice cream sundaes under moonlight.
We'll toast to sweetness, a fruity cheer,
With every bite, we hold life dear.

Rhythm of Raindrops on Tin Roofs

Pitter-patter on the roof, oh what a sound,
Raindrops tap danced on the ground.
Inside we sip our hot cocoa bliss,
While puddles outside invite a splish-splash kiss.

The cat slides by, with a sassy flair,
Pausing once, to shake off air.
Kids jump in with a splashing cheer,
While parents sigh, wishing for clear.

Board games unfold amid the storm,
Laughter erupts, a cozy warm.
Outside, the rain sings soft lullabies,
Inside, we plot our next big surprise.

So let it rain, let the droplets play,
With tin roofs drumming in a merry way.
We'll dance inside through every storm,
Creating smiles, that's the norm!

Lush Echoes of Lapping Waves

The ocean whispers secrets low,
As tiny fish put on a show.
Board shorts flutter in the salty breeze,
While everyone's trying to catch the tease.

A beach ball flies, a seagull squawks,
Sandcastles rise, but the tide mocks.
Flip-flops vanish in the deep blue,
Leaving behind just one, maybe two.

The sunset paints the sky so bright,
While folks tell tales of their day's delight.
And as the waves lap, theycheerfully crash,
We laugh aloud in this salty splash.

So join the joy of lapping waves,
In sandy nooks, our heart braves.
With waves to dance and friends so near,
Let's celebrate the fun, oh dear!

Seashells and Sunshine Smiles

Seashells giggle on the shore,
As seagulls dance and kids explore.
Sandcastles rise, a sandy throne,
With sippy cups, we're never alone.

Flip-flops flying, oh what glee,
Caught a crab, it ran from me!
Sunburned noses, laughter loud,
We'll show the tides who's really proud.

Ice cream drips and seagulls dive,
Chasing shadows, oh, alive!
We'll trade our spoons for shiny wands,
And summon waves with sandy hands.

Dreams Cradled in Coconut Cradles

Coconuts sway like gentle dreams,
Hats made of palm, or so it seems.
Toast to the coconuts at play,
As monkeys giggle and steal our spray.

Sugar drinks in big coconuts,
Dancing fronds and silly struts.
We talk to fish, they nod and sigh,
While sipping sunbeams, oh my, oh my!

Tropical storms chase us indoors,
With treasure maps and pirate boars.
We roll our eyes and start to snore,
As dreams of coconuts spin to shore.

Lanterns Glow in Palm Frond Shadows

Lanterns flicker, casting laughs,
Where shadows dance like silly calves.
Palm fronds sway, they gossip too,
Under a moon that's laughing, woo-hoo!

We sit in circles, tales to share,
With fishy jokes that fill the air.
The breeze brings whispers from the sea,
As laughter blends, just you and me.

The night's a stage for goofy sights,
With dogs in hats and silly fights.
Lanterns glow, our faces bright,
In this kingdom of pure delight.

Fragrant Plumeria in the Coastal Air

Plumeria scents drift on the breeze,
Tickling noses, making us sneeze.
Flowers in hair, a rainbow's grin,
While laughing crabs play catch and spin.

We dance like waves upon the sand,
With flip-flops flying, what a band!
The sun winks down, it knows our fun,
As we chase shadows, we're never done.

A picnic feast with sandwiches bold,
Soggy chips that we can't uphold.
But laughter bubbles, we don't care,
Fragrant plumeria fills the air.

In the Embrace of Turquoise Waters

Sunbathers bask, like lizards in the sun,
Waiting for ice cream, oh what fun.
Seagulls gossip, stealing beach snacks away,
They squawk in laughter, it's their buffet.

Splashing kids dive, they're a playful crew,
Cute little mermaids, but with less to do.
Be careful of jellyfish, and their stings,
But who knew a sting could make one sing?

Floats and rafts drift, like clouds in the air,
While belly flops create quite the flair.
With sunburned noses and goofy hats,
We giggle and laugh, just look at those chats!

As sunset whispers, the party won't stop,
We dance with shadows, hopping like a frog.
In turquoise waters, life's mishaps feel right,
With laughter and friends, we own the night.

Feast of Flora and Fauna

Palm trees sway, with a puzzled grin,
Do they talk to each other, where to begin?
Flowers bloom, in colors so bright,
Offering nectar to bees in delight.

Coconuts tumble, with a comedic flair,
Bouncing on beaches, they float through the air.
Sand crabs tiptoe, in their silly parade,
Who knew they had moves? Just watch their charade!

Parrots squawk gossip, oh such a delight,
About the rumors of fish that take flight.
Nature's own circus, with laughter and cheer,
We feast on freshness, while water's so near.

With salad of seaweed, and fruit to the brim,
We dine like kings, though the vibe is quite dim.
But when the moon rises, the laughter resumes,
At this feast of nature, we owls find our rooms.

Melodies of the Sea Breeze

Wind whistles harmonies, in whispers and shouts,
While beachcombers chase after the best clout.
Each wave brings a tune, with a splosh and a splash,
As fish join the chorus, in a bubbly bash.

Seashells echo, like instruments played,
With crabby soloists, in a promenade.
The sun sets low, with a golden blush,
While starfish dance on, in a soft little hush.

Breezes stroke skin, like a lover's soft kiss,
While blown-off hats create a funny abyss.
With laughter in the air, and joy all around,
Life's sweet serenade, the happiest sound.

As night rolls in, fireflies take flight,
Creating a ballet, in the soft moonlight.
We sway to the magic, in nature's embrace,
In melodies found, we all find our place.

Driftwood Messages

Driftwood pieces, like storytellers old,
Whispering tales, both funny and bold.
They drift from afar, with secrets to share,
But mostly they giggle, as they catch salty air.

A message in a bottle, who knows what it said?
"Where's my lunch?" on a fishy slice of bread.
With crabs as interpreters, making cheer,
They giggle at humans, way out here.

Pieces of treasures, washed up on the shore,
Each smoother than the last, with stories galore.
A shoe from a sailor, a flip-flop of grace,
Who thought driftwood sports could be such a race?

We gather our findings, with joy in our hearts,
Crafting silly stories, oh where do we start?
With driftwood messages, and laughter so grand,
Island life teaches, let fun be your plan.

Fireflies and Fishermen's Tales

Under the stars, the fish stories grow,
With each cast of lines, the laughter does flow.
A fisherman claims he caught a big whale,
But all we find is a singed orange peel.

Fireflies dance like they're part of the show,
Winking at fishermen, chasing a glow.
"I swear he was this big!" they boast and they brag,
While the truth is trapped in an old burlap bag.

A bucket of bait and a cooler of beer,
That's the secret to fillin' up the idea.
We sit by the shore, while the hours drift by,
For a good fish story is worth a good lie!

So raise up your drink to the fish that got away,
And to fireflies buzzing by night and by day.
A friend with a joke and a strange fishing tale,
Makes me believe that the ocean won't fail.

Moonlit Hues Over Tranquil Waters

The moon hangs low, casting a silver sheen,
On waters so calm, they'd make a good scene.
Yet here on the shore, with sand on my toes,
A crab pinches my leg—ah, how my luck goes!

With night's gentle breeze comes a raucous delight,
As laughter erupts, we dance through the night.
Someone's crooning a tune, off-key as can be,
While others all chirp in with a wild spaghetti.

The moonbeams giggle, sparks in our eyes,
As kite-flying kangaroos start to rise.
We toast to the night with coconut drinks,
And ponder the worlds beyond our wild pinks.

So let's not forget, as we laugh 'till we cry,
It's the memories made that can't ever die.
In moonlit hues, under tropical charms,
We find life's true compass is friendship in arms.

Breezy Paths of Lush Green Trails

Through breezy paths where the palm leaves sway,
We stumble and trip like it's comedy play.
With flip-flops squeaking, we wander with glee,
While chasing a chicken that just won't flee.

Lush trails lead us past flowers so bright,
Each bloom a giggle in morning's soft light.
"Watch out for spiders!" becomes the next shout,
As we dodge each web with a gleeful pout.

A picnic is brewing, but with ants as our guests,
They crawl to the snacks, uninvited guests!
Chasing our lunches, as laughter prevails,
In this little slice of lush, silly tales.

Among the green trails and giddy delight,
We toast to our blunders, our laughs take flight.
For what's an adventure without a small spill,
When being a fool is the best of the thrill!

Salt-Kissed Kisses at Twilight Hour

As twilight falls with a salty embrace,
We share silly kisses, boisterous and face.
Waves whisper secrets that sparkle and rush,
While seagulls make faces, all part of the hush.

With each sushi taco that we bravely munch,
We laugh till we choke on our adventurous lunch.
"Who needs utensils?" becomes our new camp,
As we dive into laughter while we munch and stamp.

The sun dips low, painting skies in fun hues,
While the evening brings us playful old blues.
The crabs roll around, doing dances so wacky,
And we join in their fun, feeling quite tacky.

At twilight hour, with kisses so bright,
We treasure the moments that make our hearts light.
For when salt-kissed laughter fills up the air,
Every silly moment is one we all share.

Fishermen's Tales at Dusk

The fishermen gather, rods in hand,
Swapping tall tales of the sea and sand.
One claims his catch was bigger than a whale,
While another insists it swam away with his ale.

They laugh and jest, as the sun starts to fade,
Casting their lines in a grand charade.
A fish leaps out, then falls with a splat,
And everyone yells, "That was a trick! Imagine that!"

Bait and laughter mix in the salty breeze,
With stories of snags and the odd rogue tease.
A trophy fish? No, just a leftover sinker,
Yet they celebrate like kings, each drink a thinker.

As dusk settles in, the stars the real prize,
Underneath their laughter, a mischief that lies.
For in the end, it's the joy, not the catch,
That brings them together, each memory a match.

Island Echoes of Joy

On golden sands where the crabs scurry,
Laughter erupts, oh what a flurry!
A child runs wild, with a bucket in hand,
Befriending a hermit, they form a band.

The sun shines bright as the waves make a splash,
Kids do a dance, while old folks just gash.
"Ouch!" says a grandma, as she lands on her rear,
But even her frown ends up turning to cheer.

Coconuts fly sharp like arrows in flight,
As pigeons plot heists in the soft summer light.
A dog steals sandwiches, makes a quick race,
Leaving behind a trail of crumbs in its chase.

At night, by the fire, shadows flicker and play,
Echoes of joy fading out the day.
With marshmallows roasting and tales that don't end,
Island after island, a change of the trend.

Swaying Palms and Saltwater Dreams

Beneath the swaying palms, a hammock is hung,
Where giddy tourists sing melodies unsung.
One sings of mermaids, with hair oh so bright,
While another just snores, oblivious to the fright.

Salty breezes carry whispers of fun,
As beach bums debate who's the best in the run.
"Who caught the biggest?" "I'm surely the one!"
Meanwhile, a seagull swoops in, steals their bun.

There's a game of beach volleyball, sandy and loud,
As they dive for the ball, causing quite the crowd.
Each tumble and trip, poses with mirth,
Gives laughter a birth, worth every ounce of worth.

As the sun dips low, the laughter still flows,
With stories of pirates that nobody knows.
Palm trees giggle as if they agree,
In the land of the sun, oh how happy they be!

Whispering Waves Beneath the Sun

The waves whisper secrets as they kiss the shore,
While beachgoers scramble for sunscreen galore.
One brave kid yells, "I can swim with the fish!"
But all he finds is a soggy old dish.

A sunbather fidgets, adjusting her hat,
While her sandwich rolls away, making a run for the fat.
A seagull swoops down, with a triumphant call,
Leaving behind a poof! Oh, the chaos of all.

Surfboards ready, and a wave fills with glee,
As surfers wobble, but who's catching me?
One tumbles backwards, shouts, "Look, I'm a star!"
While others just paddle, not going too far.

At sunset, they gather, with tales oh so wild,
Of jellyfish dances and seaweed piled.
With giggles and grins, they toast their delight,
Under whispering waves, as day fades to night.

Memories in Seashells

In a shell, I found my shoe,
No idea how it got there, too!
Crabs danced with a flick of delight,
As they practiced for a talent night.

The sunburnt tourists sunbathed wide,
While seagulls plotted a sneaky glide.
One swooped down for my sandwich stash,
Who knew they'd be such a food-loving crash!

A conch called out with a raspy croon,
Claiming it authored the sun and moon.
I laughed at how shells held such pride,
Dusting off dreams in the ocean tide.

Memories stuck like sand in my hair,
With laughs and mishaps beyond compare.
Like waves that dance upon the shore,
These tales make me wish for even more.

Castaway Stories

A parrot squawked, 'You're stuck with me!'
While I crafted a chair from a palm tree.
The crab tried stealing my coconut drink,
I let out a laugh, gave it a wink.

The tide rolled in with a joke or two,
It whispered secrets, 'But can you brew?'
As I built a raft made of flip-flops,
Winding waves acted like crazy props.

Fishing for lunch, I caught a flip-flop,
The fish called me over: 'You're a flop!'
Yet, I chuckled as lunch swam away,
Where's the buffet on this sandy bay?

The sandcastles wore crowns and capes,
While jellyfish hosted silly scrapes.
In the land of fun, lost and free,
I found my heart under the palm tree.

Flavors of the Sunset

Sipping cocktails from a coconut cup,
The sunset danced, as if to cheer up.
Mango bubbles went up in the sky,
As laughter bubbled, oh me, oh my!

The grill was hot with fish on the flame,
But somehow they all forgot my name.
The seagull stole all my fries with flair,
While I only got crumbs, this isn't fair!

Sunset sprinkled like sugar on sand,
While dancing shadows took a grand stand.
Each time I reached for a sweet little bite,
The sunset giggled, 'Oh, what a night!'

The colors weaved like a tapestry bright,
In this twilight kitchen where dreams take flight.
With laughter and flavors so bold and wide,
Even the waves would dance with pride.

The Warmth of Island Embraces

I lost my hat in a warm ocean breeze,
The fish giggled, 'Wear us, if you please!'
Palm trees waved with a jolly cheer,
As the warm sands whispered, 'Stay right here!'

My flip-flops grew legs, took a stroll,
While I chased after them, all out of control.
Coconuts laughed, a very chummy crowd,
As shells cheered on, 'Make us proud!'

Crabs in tuxedos danced on the shore,
Declaring this party the best ever more.
Island embraces wrapped us tight,
Turning odd incidents into pure delight.

With every sunset, a new tale unfolds,
Of laughter and warmth, far from the cold.
In the arms of the islands, life's simple grace,
We find joy in every clumsy embrace.

Solitude on the Shores

Seagulls squawk, they steal my lunch,
I argue back, they just won't budge.
Sand sticks to my sunscreen smear,
A crab steals my flip-flops, oh dear!

A tanned man joins me with a grin,
He's got coconut water, I can't compete.
His dance moves, oh, they spin and twirl,
While I just sit and watch the world.

Waves crash loud, a clueless fish,
It jumps right in – I make a wish.
To swim like that, so free and wild,
While I sip my drink, a silly child.

The sun dips low; I wave goodbye,
To phantom beachgoers, they pass by.
Tomorrow brings another chance,
To laugh at life's quirky beach dance.

Footprints in the Soft Sand

My footprints follow, oh what a sight,
But then, I trip! It's quite the plight.
Waves wash in, erase my trace,
A reminder of my clumsy grace.

I spot a jellyfish, glaring bright,
Say hi to it; it's quite the fright!
Sandy dogs run, tails in the air,
They dig for treasures with such flair.

Children laugh, they build a moat,
While I ponder how they float.
Right beside them, with a silly grin,
I wave my hands, let the fun begin!

But oh! My sandwich flies away,
The wind's a joker, come what may.
I guess the gulls have made a pact,
With sandy snacks—this is a fact.

Hibiscus Hues and Ocean Blues

In a garden bright, with blooms of cheer,
I wear a shirt that's loud, oh dear!
Hibiscus petals spill like laughter,
While bees buzz matchmaking—a real disaster!

The ocean waves come crashing fast,
They tickle my toes, a cold contrast.
I try to run, but slips abound,
Splashing water, laughter's the sound.

Shell collecting, oh what a game,
But every find is a little lame.
I show a rock, call it a pearl,
The tides roll in; I give a twirl!

Umbrella drinks come with tiny straws,
I feel like royalty, with no flaws.
But sip too fast, and I might choke,
Spitting out ice with every poke.

Nostalgia in the Breeze

The wind whispers secrets of days gone by,
As I catch a whiff of coconut pie.
My grandma's laugh, it echoes near,
While I try to build, a sand fortress here.

A funky hat sits on my brow,
I'm quite the sight, but who cares now?
The clock ticks slow, not a worry in sight,
I'm living the dream, oh what a delight!

Children play tag, their joy so bright,
While I forget how to kite, oh what a fright!
With each gust, it takes to the sky,
I chase it down, oh my, oh my!

The sunset glows; I bid adieu,
To sandcastle dreams that never grew.
Tomorrow's tide brings tales anew,
And laughter will follow like morning dew.

Island-Echoed Poems

In the shade where coconuts sway,
Lemurs hide and giggle all day.
Crabs in tuxedos, dancing with pride,
While sunburned tourists slip, then glide.

Frisbees fly past the side of my head,
I wish I got a better thread.
But laughter rolls like waves so wild,
Even my sunscreen's not well-defined.

Every sip of my coconut milk,
Tastes smoother than silk, like a cuddle from a quilt.
Yet watch out for the seagulls' dive,
With crumbs in hand, you barely survive!

As the sun dips below the sea,
Fishes tell tales to the bamboo tree.
So let's dance like jellyfish in the tide,
And wave goodbye with the crabs at our side.

Coastal Hues of Pomegranate Red

Painted skies, a strawberry hue,
Laughter sounds like a tropical brew.
Mangoes drop low, on the ocean's crest,
While parrots gossip, as if this is a quest.

Picnics of sandwiches, a breaded defeat,
The seagulls swoop in, can't help but cheat.
Life jackets float like marshmallows near,
Let's play pirate, but keep legs sincere!

The beach ball rolls, then falls from a glee,
My flip-flop's a catapult, catch me if you see!
Sandy toes and sunburned knees,
Join our game, bring along some breeze!

As tides retreat, we dance in the sand,
Doing the conga—come join the band!
So cheers with pineapple in our right hand,
Because laughter and sun, oh isn't life grand?

Spectacle of a Seaside Escape

Monkeys surf on tiny boards,
Making waves like cartoon lords.
My sunscreen's stubborn, like a grumpy cat,
But a handstand's fun, or so they say at that!

Shells become hats, put them to the test,
I'm a seashell prince, feeling quite blessed.
Flip-flops flying, a tournament of sorts,
Beach volleyball with coconut courts!

Sandy snacks and drinks so sweet,
Alligators styled in flip-flops on their feet.
Barefoot strolling, we slip and slide,
While the sunset paints our crazy ride.

Musical crabs tap on the rocks,
As we twirl to the sound of laughter's clocks.
Fun and folly on this sunny stage,
Life's a joke we all engage.

Feast on the Fragrance of Paradise

Picnic spread on a checkered cloth,
Limes and laughter, caught in a froth.
Kites in the sky, upside-down delight,
While a dog steals my sandwich with a bite.

Breezes whisper like gossips in bloom,
Swaying palm trees, the sun's golden room.
Sipping piña coladas, I spill my cheer,
The bartender smirks, his grin so sincere.

Seashells line up for their fashion show,
Baring all secrets, in a sun-glow bow.
Jumping into waves, I may lose my hat,
But who needs a hat when the ocean's like that?

Yachts bobbing gently—a floating parade,
Island tunes played, my cares start to fade.
With each silly moment, the sun starts to set,
This feast of joy? I'll never forget!

Caribbean Castaways under Starlit Skies

We found a coconut by the shore,
It stared at us, wanting more.
With every sip, we'd laugh and grieve,
Did it hold treasure or just leave?

Our boat was made of driftwood pie,
It wobbled much, oh me, oh my!
We thought we'd sail to far-off lands,
But here we are, with empty cans!

A stingray stole my soggy hat,
I chased it down; how dare that brat!
The fish all laughed; they threw a show,
I'm now the village clown, you know!

Under bright moons, we sing and twirl,
With wild seaweed, I take a whirl.
Life's a dance with sandy feet,
In our lost home, oh so sweet!

Whispered Secrets of the Wind

The palm trees talk with rustling leaves,
I swear I caught a tale of thieves!
A parrot squawked, 'Oh, what a day!'
We laughed as wind tossed us away.

A crab marched by in fancy shoes,
With tiny socks, he showed his moves.
We cheered him on, a dance so grand,
In this odd world, we took a stand!

The breeze plays tricks; it pulls my hair,
Is it the wind, or just my scare?
As sea foam tickles all around,
We're silly souls, on joy unbound!

With every gust, a joke is told,
In this paradise, we feel so bold.
We gather shells to make a throne,
But really, it's just a comfy zone!

Serendipity in Sandy Footprints

I lost my shoe upon the sand,
A crab claimed it, his throne so grand.
With every step, my toes did dance,
To find that shoe, I'd not take a chance!

Sunburned noses, bright and red,
The local cows, they laugh instead.
They glance at us with their big eyes,
As if to say, 'What a surprise!'

We built a castle, tall and wide,
But at high tide, we had to hide.
It crumbled down, much like our plans,
Who knew wet sand could take our stands?

Footprints lead where laughter's spun,
Chasing waves, oh what fun!
Life's just wacky, full of quirks,
In every grain, adventure lurks!

Bounty of the Sea

My fishing pole's a garden rake,
I caught a seaweed, for goodness' sake!
With every cast, I lose my edge,
But hey, at least it's quite a pledge!

The fish parade with fancied scales,
They gossip 'bout our silly tales.
One tried to nibble on my toes,
Said I was tasty, goodness knows!

Bring out the nets, let's catch a feast,
Or maybe just a soggy beast.
With every dish, there's laughter here,
Gourmet meals, or fishy cheer!

Sea cucumbers in coconut stew,
Throw in some laughter, and we're through.
Life in the ocean's full of glee,
Even if I'mjust a wannabe!

Gifts from the Depths

The ocean's deep, with treasures rare,
A ship's lost sock, or was it a chair?
With diving gear, I take the plunge,
To fetch up things that make me grunge!

A friendly dolphin took a glance,
Invited me to join his dance.
With bubbles floating all around,
We twirled and laughed, oh what a sound!

Coral castles, bright and bold,
With secrets whispered, never told.
An octopus played poker there,
Lost all his chips, did we care?

I surfaced up, what a delight,
With fishy friends that swim in sight.
From depths below, to skies so bright,
Life's a riddle, full of light!

Passionfruit and Paradise Found

In the market, fruits on parade,
Passionfruit smiles, or so I've made!
Sipping juice with a straw that's bent,
Life's a game—I'm the main event!

Coconuts dance, shaking their heads,
While pineapples sit on their golden beds.
I fumble, I trip, on bananas I slip,
In paradise, laughter's the best kind of rip!

Seagulls circle, with sass and flair,
Stealing snacks while I sit and stare.
A crab skitters by, in shorts too tight,
Waving his claws, what a comical sight!

Under the sun, every moment's a jest,
With fruity delights, I feel so blessed.
In this tropical whirl, I dance and I spin,
Every day here, I'm destined to win!

Serenities of Seafoam and Sand

A beach umbrella flops in the breeze,
While kids dig holes that swallow their knees.
I build a sandcastle, it's an awkward sight,
When a wave crashes down—oh, what a fright!

Seashells conspire, plotting my doom,
As I trip on a flip-flop—there's chaos and gloom!
Seagulls are laughing, they think it's a game,
I'm just here hoping they'll remember my name!

My sunscreen's a beacon, so bright and white,
A sticky mess that's a true blight!
The sand's in my sandwich, oh what a treat,
Each bite's like a crunch of grainy defeat!

As the sun sets low, the sky turns to gold,
I'm dragging my cooler, it's heavy and cold.
Yet in this grand chaos, one thing is true,
Island antics will always renew!

Tidal Rhythms & Aquatic Whispers

The tide rolls in with a giggle and roar,
Laughing at treasures washed up on the shore.
A fish flops around, in a dance it weaves,
While I'm tangled in seaweed, clutching my keys!

The waves play tag with my toes as I run,
A sand crab decides that I'm way more fun.
"Let's race!" I yell, but he's already won,
With a crabby little chortle, he'll bask in the sun!

Whispers of dolphins in playful delight,
Throwing back jokes 'til the stars are in sight.
Their splashes send me, tumbling back,
Me and my sandwich, it's a slippery snack!

Under the moon, the ocean's my friend,
With laughter and waves that never do end.
In this splashy ballet, I twirl and I spin,
Each pulse of the sea brings more giggles within!

Dunes Dressed in Sunlit Green

The dunes are alive, with giggles galore,
As I race past the ferns, towards sandy decor.
I trip, I roll, in the green and the gold,
Mountain of laughter, this story unfolds!

Lizards are sunbathing, giving me shade,
While I try to stay cool, in a hat that's handmade.
A breeze lifts my drink, oh what a cruel tease—
I'm chasing a coconut with all of my knees!

In the brush, a parrot squawks out a tune,
Dancing on branches, he's quite the buffoon.
With bright colored feathers, he struts with a flair,
Just like my uncle, though he doesn't compare!

As shadows grow long, the laughter's still bright,
I'll toast to the dunes, and the day's last light.
In this mischief of green, I'm free to explore,
Island adventures make my spirit soar!

Stories Woven in Coral Sand

Under the sun, where crabs do dance,
A flip-flop's fate is a rare chance.
With beach balls bouncing, oh what a sight,
As seagulls squawk in pure delight.

Fishermen fish with nets so wide,
While kids on floats go for a ride.
The sandcastle stands, but watch out,
A wave's come crashing, gone without doubt!

Waves will whisper tales of old,
Of treasure chests and pirates bold.
But here on shore, we just snack fries,
And laugh at seagulls with their sly eyes.

So grab a drink, let worries flee,
In this sandy realm, we're all so free.
With watermelon slices, joy we find,
Let's share stories, and ease our mind.

The Lullaby of Lapping Water

The tide hums softly, a gentle cheer,
As dolphins dance, never did we fear.
A crab in sunglasses strolls on by,
Winking at tourists under the sky.

Seagulls gossip about last night's loot,
While fish swim fast, in a swift pursuit.
The coconut drinks, foam on the rim,
Raise to cheers, let the laughter brim!

Sun-kissed cheeks and laughter spread wide,
In the hammock's sway, we try to hide.
But sway we do, we giggle and fall,
A tumble of joy, we answer the call.

One palm tree leans, just to have fun,
With its coconuts dropping, oh what a run!
The lapping water sings, sweet and clear,
In this paradise, who needs a career?

Sips of Tropical Joy and Serenity

Mango smoothies with a bit of zing,
A toast to the sun and the joy it brings.
With silly straws and mini umbrellas,
We smile at passersby, happy fella!

Pineapple pizza – yes, it's a thing,
Even the dolphins can't help but sing.
As waves crash down, ice cream we chase,
Laughing out loud, it's a grand race!

Palm trees sway as if to the beat,
Dancing around with wiggly feet.
Just sip and giggle, let worries fade,
In the land where happiness is made.

With every sip, we live so bold,
Sharing stories, laughter, and tales untold.
A tropical breeze carries our cheer,
In this crazy life, we have no fear.

Whispers of Laughter in the Breeze

The breeze carries whispers of joy and fun,
Where neighbors compete in a coconut run.
With hats on heads and sunscreen slathered,
We giggle together, our worries shattered.

Bamboo huts sway, laughter spills wide,
As kids play tag, trying to hide.
A parrot squawks, thinking it's grand,
Spilling secrets, just as we planned.

With each splash and snack on the sand,
Life feels like a dance, perfectly planned.
Fried plantains served with a side of glee,
In this little nook, we're fancy and free!

So let's recount the jokes we've spun,
Under this sky where life's pure fun.
When laughter drifts in, we'll all believe,
In island life, where laughter won't leave.

Island Whispers

In flip-flops that squeak on the sand,
I strut like a crab, feeling quite grand.
The palm trees giggle at my tan lines,
While seagulls steal chips — oh, how unkind!

My sunscreen's a puzzle, a real sticky trap,
Covered in lotion, I napped on my lap.
A wave crashes in, my sandwich now wet,
Wet bread and regrets, my best splash yet!

The fish in the sea think they're quite sly,
Teasing my hook as I sigh and I try.
"I'm just here for laughter!" I shout to the sky,
But the gulls take my fries - oh me, oh my!

Drifting on floats shaped like flamingo,
With a drink in my hand, just taking it slow.
My best friend's a crab, so we share all our woes,
He chats with the shells, where the gossip flows.

Sunlit Shores and Salted Air

Sunshine ricochets off my shiny bald head,
While I chase the kids, but they're always ahead.
Building sand castles that collapse with a flop,
Shouting "Watch out!" as I trip and I drop!

The beach ball has wings, it flies like a kite,
And lands on my face — what a comical sight!
The sand's in my hair, and I can't find my shoe,
A snack's in the cooler, but it feels like a zoo.

With a drink in my hand and a smile so wide,
I try to look cool, but I'm slipping in tide.
The ocean's a giggle, it roars with delight,
As I tumble and splutter, oh what a fright!

The sunset's a postcard, and I'm in the frame,
With laughter and joy, I will stake my claim.
Tomorrow I'll swim, but for now, I'll just chill,
Wrapped up in my towel, it's a beachy thrill!

The Rhythm of Gentle Waves

The waves dance in rhythm like a clumsy band,
I try to keep time, but I can't understand.
With a splash and a laugh, I face the great blue,
While dodging the seaweed — oh, what a view!

The jellyfish jiggle, they wave me to play,
But I back away slowly, keeping fears at bay.
"Hey, don't sting me!" I shout, with a laugh and a spin,
They just float by, and I'm left in my skin.

My towel's a blanket, a nest on the shore,
Sandy sandwiches, who could ask for more?
A flip of my flop sends a friend for a fall,
As laughter erupts like a shore's loud call.

With a bucket in hand, I collect all the shells,
Each one's a story that nature tells.
I'll take them all home, a treasure to keep,
Mixed in with the giggles, inside my heart deep.

Coconut Dreams

A coconut dream, just roll with the flow,
With a grin on my face, I'm the star of the show.
A sip from the shell, it's a tropical brew,
But my straw just broke — oh, what can I do?

The breeze whispers low, like a cheeky old friend,
While I dance with the waves, just hoping they'll bend.
The locals all laugh as I trip and I slip,
It's hard to look cool when you're always a grip!

With conga lines forming, I give it a go,
Swinging my hips — oh, hey, watch that toe!
The music's contagious, the sand welcomes feet,
In a whirl of pure joy, this life's quite a treat!

As night settles down, I gaze at the stars,
Each twinkle a memory, it's healing my scars.
With coconut dreams, I drift into sleep,
Awash with the laughter that I'll always keep.

Tides of Tranquility

The waves come in and out with cheer,
Sunburned noses all gather near.
Flip-flops flying, oh what a sight,
As seagulls squawk, they join the fight.

In a beach chair, I nap like a pro,
Sandy snacks stacked in a row.
Crab cakes dancing, they steal the show,
While tourists decide which way to go.

Shells and stories, a treasure hunt,
Flip that crab, the skills you'll flaunt!
But watch your drink! A seagull dive,
To steal your joy, oh look alive!

The sunset glows, the fun won't end,
With goofy jokes, we all pretend.
Life's a breeze, with laughter sweet,
As flamingos join our happy beat.

Laughter Beneath the Palms

Underneath the palms we play,
Witty banter leads the way.
Beach ball bouncing, laughter flies,
Check your hat before it dies!

Sipping cocktails, we toast the day,
But who switched mine? I must say!
Pineapple hats, quite the delight,
Making island mischief at night.

Seashells giggling as we dance,
Mermaid dreams in a funny trance.
Flip-flops squeaking, we all trip,
Watch out for that banana slip!

With coconut drinks and grins so wide,
We just can't seem to hide our pride.
Island life, it's pure and bright,
Making memories, oh what a sight!

Emerald Coves and Coral Shadows

Emerald waters call us close,
With coral shadows, we shall boast.
Fins and flippers dive and dash,
Mermaid sightings? Oh, what a splash!

Surfboards wobble, oh what a feat,
Balance like we're on shaky feet.
Shells hold secrets, whispers rare,
"Was that a fish?" we gasp in the air.

Picnic spreads in the afternoon sun,
Sandwiches emptied, but we've had fun.
Pineapple juice spills on the floor,
Laughing at crabs who've come for more.

As dusk arrives, lanterns float,
Stories shared, we giggle and gloat.
Emerald cove, our hearts do swell,
With all our antics, who needs a shell?

Serenity on a Sandy Canvas

Brightly colored kites fly high,
As we wave to clouds drifting by.
Splashing water with each bold leap,
Watch the sandcastles slowly weep!

Picnics packed with love and cheer,
"Who brought the napkins?" someone sneers.
Sandwiches staged like fine cuisine,
If only seagulls weren't so mean!

Beachcombers search with hopeful glee,
Twisting their toes, just wait and see.
Finding treasures buried deep,
The laughter echoes, oh, what a leap!

As the sun sets, we make a wish,
For more adventures, that's our dish.
Serenity reigns but it's not so neat,
With giggles and spills, oh what a feat!

Festivals of Color in the Island Sun

Banners wave, the drums they boom,
Dancers in bright skirts fill the room.
Everyone's laughing, faces aglow,
Who knew a fish could steal the show?

Pineapple hats and neon shades,
Sipping punch while on parades.
The roasted goat, it gives a cheer,
But it's the coconut float that draws us near!

Laughter echoes through palm trees,
Jokes fly freely, carried on the breeze.
A crab joins in, winks at the crowd,
Dancing sideways, oh so proud!

When the sun sets, we share a hug,
Tales of mischief, a friendly tug.
Under the stars, we sing and play,
Who cares if the rooster joins the fray?

Vibrations of Nature in Open Waters

Kayaks rolling with a splashy cheer,
Fishies giggling as they swim near.
The seaweed dances, swaying around,
Even the crabs are pulling pranks, profound!

With surfboards flying and waves galore,
We try to catch waves, but mostly just score.
A dolphin jumps, gives us a grin,
'You call that surfing? Just dive right in!'

Seagulls squawk, stealing our fries,
While we laugh until we cry.
A shark in a tux, oh what a sight!
Just trying to crash our beach party tonight!

As the tide changes, we surf and we slide,
Riding that wave, we take it in stride.
Nature's laughter, a brilliant surprise,
With each whimsical splash, our spirits rise!

Clamshells and Coconut Gatherings

Cracked coconuts and clamshells galore,
We feast like kings, hear the island lore.
The salty breeze and giggles collide,
While seagulls argue who's got the best ride!

Gather 'round, it's a clam chowder toss,
Who'll be the champion, or will we all loss?
With each splatter, we burst into tears,
Laughter's the spice as we banish our fears!

The parrot's cheeky, repeating our glee,
Mocking our voices, oh can't you see?
Grab a coconut, take a big swing,
Watch it explode — oh, what fun it brings!

As night falls over this festive scene,
We toast to our antics, holding our keen.
With memories made under twinkling stars,
We'll always remember these coconut wars!

Island Heartbeat: The Pulse of Paradise

In the island's heart, rhythm does reign,
With every swish, we forget our pain.
Drumming up fun as we twist and shout,
Even the iguanas are wiggling out!

Every sunset brings a brand new tune,
Sand between toes, the silver moon.
The ocean whispers, 'Come dance with me!',
Little fish jump, as happy as can be!

Rum-soaked adventures, giggles galore,
Jumping in waves, always wanting more.
Our laughter mingles with the sea breeze,
Living our lives with absolute ease!

With each pulse, we bring forth bright sun,
The island life knows how to have fun.
So let's toast to joy, with a wink and grin,
For in paradise, the laughter won't thin!

Odyssey of the Ocean's Embrace

Waves whisper secrets, fish tell jokes,
Sunburned tourists, with iced drinks and pokes.
Seagulls squawk, stealing chips from your hand,
A crab in the sand sings in a rock band.

Palm trees sway, doing the hula dance,
While locals sip rum, giving you a glance.
A conch shell rings, but the message is clear,
Forget your worries, just laugh and be near.

Flip-flops flapping, kids chasing a kite,
There's no such thing as a wrong or right sight.
Sandcastles crumble, but spirits won't drown,
As laughter erupts, masking any frown.

Rustic Boats and Tranquil Sounds

Old wooden boats creak, with tales to unfold,
Fishermen laughing, their stories are gold.
Baiting their hooks with a chuckle or two,
Fish are elusive—oh, the ones that got away, boo!

Tranquility reigns, yet madness abounds,
As tourists get towel-whipped, true joy knows no bounds.

Drifting in dreams, one feels like a star,
On a floating stronghold, trapped in a jar.

A dolphin appears, showcasing its flair,
While kids splash around, without a single care.
Wildlife, they roar—oh, it's quite a scene,
As laughter unites, and we all feel serene.

Harboring Dreams at Sunset's Edge

The horizon is painted with hues of delight,
As the sunset giggles, wrapping day in night.
Barbecues firing; the smells fill the air,
With laughter like music, as if without care.

Each drink clinks loudly, a toast to the dusk,
To the spontaneous games and the unplanned husk.
Someone slips in, it's not the first time,
Yet everyone joins in, giving it a rhyme.

Anchors are lifted, but spirits won't sink,
As tales are spun over cups filled with pink.
Memories grow, like the waves in the bay,
As we harbor our dreams, come what may.

Cobalt Waters

Cobalt blue dances beneath the sun's gaze,
Mermaids and mermen bask, lost in a daze.
A paddleboard tumbles, with laughter so bright,
A fish giggles softly at our silly plight.

Flippers and fins shape a riotous scene,
As children discover what the ocean's mean.
The sea turtles glide, with elegance grand,
While humor floats softly, like waves on the sand.

Shells play percussion, the crabs tap their feet,
The rhythm of ocean life—oh isn't it sweet!
Jellyfish waltz as the sun takes a dip,
In cobalt waters, we all lose our grip.

www.ingramcontent.com/pod-product-compliance
Lightning Source LLC
Chambersburg PA
CBHW072222070526
44585CB00015B/1446